Eternal Seconds

Eternal

Seconds

A Poetry Collection of Longing

Andrew Chiniche

Reflective
Light
Press

Eternal Seconds by Andrew Chiniche

Published by Reflective Light Press
Copyright © 2022 Andrew Chiniche

First Edition: February 2022
Printed in the United States of America

Paperback ISBN: 978-0-578-35448-4
Hardback ISBN: 978-1-7326824-9-8

Edited by Eva Zen
Cover by Frina Art

Another moment escapes.

Notice that nothing changes.

Never give up hope.

Another chance will appear...

First Lines

Reflections

00:59

I elevate you
into the realm of the fantastic
and release a prayer to the Goddess.

May she allow us to be reunited.
I need the magick of your presence.

00:58

Remember the way time slowed
when we played together
in the rooms of debauchery?

I hope the miles
between us shrink to inches.

Only then can we travel
to the edge of oblivion.

00:57

The world disappears
in colorful pulsating stage lights
as the beat of dance music mesmerizes.

A cocoon of desire surrounds us
and we transcend into the tangible moment.
My fingers trace the curve of your hip
to follow the glisten of your skin.

My blood boils,
and I devour you with my eyes.

With a snap of elastic
and a slight caress,
a tribute is made.

I feel the warmth of the sun in your smile
and see eternity expand
in the solar system of your eyes.

00:56

The Goddess' strength never buckles;
it shines and inspires.

You are Her!

Embrace your beauty
by releasing your inhibitions,
and show your power
through seductive touch.

Explode your effervescent light
to the world
and be my beacon.

00:55

Visions of you dance
with the musical memory
of Sexy M.F.'s pulsating beat.

As I escape the stress of life,
the delicious curves of your body
spin and rotate to defy gravity.

The fiery passion of your eyes
flash with the universal secret,
and infuse my senses with magick.

00:54

As I miss the pillowy caress of your lips,
my mind fills with a memory of delight:

You float to me from the darkness,
wrap me in your arms,
and whisper,
"Hello".

The heat of your body
radiates with each beat of your heart,
and anchors me to your essence.

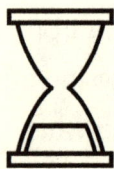

00:53

There is a majesty and grace
in the flow of your body.

Your magick's radiance
takes my breath away.

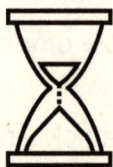

00:52

In the scope of eternity,
our time apart is less than an eye-blink.

I thank fate and the string of destiny
that our paths crossed one lonely evening.

I feel our love overflow
and consume my soul.

You are the everlasting one,
and the fulfillment of my heart's desire.

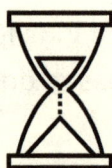

00:51

I feel your gaze over my torso.
I feel your breath on my neck.
I feel your kiss on my lips.

A surge of electricity
bursts through my limbs
and tingles to the tips of my digits.

The stars in your eyes
lift me to a new universe.

00:51

I feel your gaze over my torso.
I feel your breath on my neck.
I feel your kiss on my lips.

A surge of electricity
bursts through my limbs
and tingles to the tips of my digits.

The stars in your eyes
lift me to a new universe.

00:50

Since I cannot hold you
and whisper your in ear,
I must send you a note:

You are beautifully wonderful!

00:49

Goodnight, sweetheart!

As I drift towards sleep,
my thoughts settle on you.

We meet in the realm of Dream
as intertwined lovers,
and live off one another's essence.

Do you feel the sensation
of my lips caressing yours
in a soul-searching kiss?

00:48

I sing your praises to heaven.
I am ecstatic you exist.

With a soft whisper, I reach out
and try to elevate your day.

The weight of your being
fills the pool of my spirit.

00:47

As an unexplainable part of my soul,
I love the glorious spread of your smile,
the majestic shape of your nose,
and the velvet feel of your lips.

Most of all,
I love the power of your kindness.

00:46

Whenever I write,
whether it is about you or not,
I feel your essence
vibrate through my psyche
and influence my creativity.

You are powerful.
You are electric.
You are my fountainhead.

00:45

I miss the eager nervous energy
that coursed through my veins
as I waited for you to appear.

After your materialization,
the glow of your features
causes me to take an extra moment.

The time we spent together,
a fleeting eternity.

The moments encompassed eternal joy
but seemed to end too quickly.

You are the flame
that I want to burn in.

I cannot wait for the gulf of time and space
to collapse and alleviate our distance.

You are eternally in my heart.

00:44

In a world filled with waking dreams,
I always see you.

The fire of your eyes follows me
with the traveling sun.

The whisper of your voice
skates through the trees in a silent breeze.

Life would have less spark without you.
You make everything vivid and crisp.

Since there is no way to calculate your worth,
I hope these few words are enough.

May they lift you as you raise my soul.

00:43

To wallow in your beauty
would be heaven.

To kiss you
would be ecstatic.

To assimilate your spark
would be everlasting.

00:42

I am driven to anoint you with my love.
These words pale in comparison to what I feel,
but they are all I have.

I watch as their oil glistens over your curves
and highlights your muscles.

With a heightened anticipation,
I wait for your honeyed gaze to fall upon me.
Only then do I feel the benediction of their fire.

You speak my name,
and I hear the song of angels.

Let us merge our souls
and leave the mundane in the mud.

00:41

After lighting a taper on the altar,
I take you in my arms and kiss you:

Once for the past,
twice for the present,
thrice for our future.

The priestess binds our hands in a sacred knot
while whispering an incantation:

*"As the light of the moon glows over this couple,
may they be rewarded with the Goddess' grace
and always be in her favor."*

She seals her blessing with jasmine incense.

Our essence melds together,
and I feel a calm peace
descend upon my soul.

00:40

I cannot think of love
without being visited by a vision of you.

The warm longing attached to my core
bubbles to the surface
and erupts with lava.

I do not fight this primal urge;
I wallow in it;
I need it to propel me to greatness.

Your beauty feeds my creative impulse.
When I shape words into sentences,
I touch your body and kiss your lips.

I hear you moan my name in a whisper
and feel your nails claw across my back.
My desire for you is palpable.

I want my words formed into your naked flesh,
so I can hold you in my arms
and partake of your communion.

00:39

I dream of loving you:
a night of slow passion,
playful touching,
and deep-kissing.

Take my hand
and guide me to your sweet spot.

I want to hear you moan
and see you shiver with pleasure.

Let us wrap our naked bodies together
and talk about life,
our dreams,
and the future.

The heat of your skin on mine
is the ultimate indulgence.

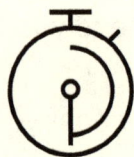

00:38

I have said this before
in different ways,
but it bears repeating:

I love you.
I Love You!
I LOVE YOU!

00:37

I feel the cold loneliness of nighttime
creep over me, and I wish for you.

You are the glow
on the edge of my horizon.
Your touch is worth everything.

Reach out to me
and let me hold you—
just for a little while…

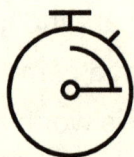

00:36

As I retreat from the world,
my thoughts hover over you.

You are life's allure,
and because I love you,
it lives within me.

I wonder what it would be like
to wake next to you,
to hold you,
to bask in your grace...

You are my hope
and my future.

I need your essence
to enliven me.

00:35

As a comet on the outer
fringe of the universe,
my molten body hurls
through time and space.

Your heart's gravity draws me closer.

With the gleam of your smile
radiating in my imagination,
the faint flicker
of your inner sun brings rapture.

Distance is meaningless
to connected souls.

00:34

I hunger for the caress of your lips,
the heat of your body,
and the sparkle of your eyes.

To think of you is magickal.

When I breathe deeply,
I feel the beat of your heart
and the flow of your blood.

I did not know love
until I knew you…

00:33

I follow Hope's water
and discover the spring of you.

As I drink from your stream,
I am nourished.

The nuance of your contours is eternal
and fills the void of time.

Let us join our lifelines in clasped palms
and bolster our forever.

00:32

I thought about picking a purple petunia
and putting it in a vase,
but this exquisiteness is fleeting
when compared with your face.

To cultivate my love,
I think of you every day.
I really want to hold you;
that is what I pray.

00:31

Come to me in the burgeoning darkness.
The shadow of a candle's flame dances
over your face and caresses your curves.

Come to me and shed your outer later.
Use the pulsing back beat
and let your clothes fall to the floor.

Come to me and straddle my lap.
Grind your pelvis into mine
while I fondle your flesh
with feather-like touches.

Come to me and kiss my soul.
Transfer your essence into me
as you trace my pulsating hardness.

Come to me and perform magick.
Teach me love, passion,
and the fulfillment of life.

Come to me.
Come with me.

00:30

As the combustion of the sun feeds itself,
my love for you grows—
a complicated filament structure
that glows from its internal heat.

You are the morning star,
and the bringer of light.
There is wisdom in this knowledge
without which all would be darkness.

I look forward to the celebration of flesh
and the bestowing of secret knowledge.

I wait in my crystal cave as eons flow.
Lost time will be restored
when I return to your arms.

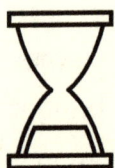

00:29

I reach into the universe
and wrap my arms around you.

I squeeze tight.

We trade the rhythm of our breathing
and enter a sensual calm.

The world disappears and leaves us.
Equal breaths inhale and exhale.

As the complexities
of our psyche collapses,
our essence intertwines
to form an endless spiral;
the loop of Love's energy.

Let us live here perpetually and prosper.

00:28

I love loving you
and I remember
the caress of your touch.

Let your aura's radiance
bounce off the stratosphere
so I may absorb
the transmission of your spirit
and know completeness.

00:27

The time has come
to celebrate the rebirth of light.

With the blizzard raging,
weave your fingers into mine,
nestle your head into my shoulder,
and hold me tight.

When I am with you,
time stretches like elastic
and everlasting happiness grows.

My hope is for you
to be my constant girl.

00:27

The time has come
to celebrate the rebirth of light.

With the blizzard raging,
weave your fingers into mine,
nestle your head into my shoulder,
and hold me tight.

When I am with you,
time stretches like elastic
and everlasting happiness grows.

My hope is for you
to be my constant girl.

00:26

The ebb and flow of my universe
rests on the shore of your elegance.

Your curves are graceful hills
across a meadow,
peaceful and serene.

In the liquid fire of your eyes
lives hypnotic enchantment.
I could get lost there for eternity…

With a glancing touch of your fingers,
electricity courses through my skin.

Surround me in your power
and never me let go.

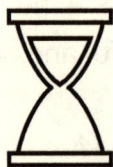

00:25

I find my thoughts turning to you…

I miss the magick of your touch
and the power of your smile.

Hugging you surrounds me
with an aura of comfort.

I pour my love into the air
and hope you feel its warmth.

00:24

The conflagration of your glamor
grows in my heart.
This everlasting fire
begets awe and excitement.

As you transcend time and space,
distance collapses
and I feel you in my arms.

To love you is the ultimate joy,
and I love you more every day.

00:23

As I huddle in the early morning darkness,
I wait for the dawn of your brilliance
to radiate upon me.

The night is cold and lonely,
but I know you will wrap me
in your embrace again.

The thread of your essence
intertwines around my heart,
and we are connected through the aether.

00:22

With our attachment to the oversoul,
we leave mortal life behind
and become God.

All time and space surrounds us.

There is no future or past,
just the everlasting now.

Join me and bask
in the glory of love.

00:21

I sing the song of you
and rejoice in your existence.

We intermingle in the stratosphere
and dance on sunbeams.

Whisper to me on the breeze
and caress me with your breath.

To love you is unlimited
and the ultimate grail.

00:20

I look at your picture
and dream about holding you:

*A fuzzy blanket wrapping around us
keeps out the cold.*

*The TV babbles with our favorite program
as I snuggle into your neck.
Your hair tickles my nose.*

*I feel your breathing steady
as you sink into comfort.*

I hope to never let you go…

00:19

Your countenance is an infinite sweetness
that continually calls me.

You are magick
and the basis of my religion.

Why look to the sky for God,
when all I need to do is look inward
and towards you.

Our essences swirl around and mix
in the recesses of our souls.

Love is eternal,
and I will love you endlessly.

00:18

Although you walk with the step of a cat,
the weight of your presence opens my eyes.

Blinking the sleep away,
I murmur into the darkness.
"Welcome home, darling. I've missed you."

The curves of your silhouette
dances across the wall.

With the whisper of fabric,
clothing peels and thumps into a hamper.

You snake underneath the quilt
and shimmy your body
into the recesses of mine.

Naked warmth chases
away the winter cold.

Our tongues dance in a sensual kiss.
Under the guidance of your fingers,

my hardness grows.

We partake in rhythmic communion
and call the elder gods with our passion.

Love's cocoon surrounds us
as we drift together
in the grasp of Morpheus.

00:17

Your beauty is reflected in the curves
and sharpness of your name.

With a faint whisper,
I taste each syllable
as it forms on my tongue.

An immortal aura surrounds you,
and it has drawn me since we met.

I reflect on that night,
and it replays like flashes of lightning,
electrifying and bright.

I wait for the miracle of reunion,
so I can once again feel the rush of blood
and the quickening of my heart.

00:16

To not love you is impossible.
Even when not thinking about you,
you live on the fringe of my thoughts.

There is a grandeur about you
bigger than the universe.
You are the queen of my everything.

00:15

The thread of life pulses through you;
a slow steady beat
full of wonderment and grace.

Let it wrap around you
and squeeze you tight.

The power of love is life,
and you encompass my love.

I desire to celebrate you
throughout my days.

I want to lift you up
and watch God radiate from your soul.

00:14

Our minds intertwine
when our bodies cannot.

Our thoughts meet in a soft kiss.
We dance on the rays of the sun
and revel in the heat of its fire.

Our all-consuming passion devours us
and brings our love to a boil.

Through the oblivion of flesh,
we ascend to a higher level
and commune with the eternal secret.

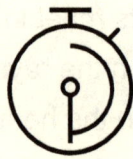

00:13

Like a flare shooting across the sky,
your beauty is a transcendent beacon.

When the distance between us shrinks,
I will wrap you in my arms,
feel the beating of your heart
and your breath on my neck.

I will drown in your kisses
and celebrate love.

There is perfection in dreams,
and I hope to join mine with yours.

00:12

Is it too much to love from afar?

A vision of you floats before me,
and a rush of passion floods my veins.

As I bask in your radiance,
happiness bubbles with translucent thoughts.

An ethereal presence surrounds
you like an aura.

You are the pinnacle of my existence;
I cannot wait to be grounded in your embrace.

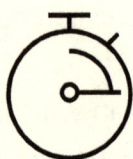

00:11

As a sister of the moon
and daughter of the sun,
you've inherited an ancient power.

From a sacred sacrifice
in the center of a faerie ring,
to dancing in the temple of the goddess,
magick lives in your bones.

Use your mental strength
and physical endurance to shape the world.
Your importance is august.

You are the shaper of lives,
and I am your poet.

00:10

If I could rewind the clock,
I would meet you again
for the first time

where we could test the other with small talk and
discover a world of secret desire;

a little universe where nothing exists,
except the soft sigh of your lips
and the smooth caress of naked flesh;

a fertile soil for the seed of love
to be planted and to thrive.

This moment lives persistently
along the perimeter of my memory.

It's amazing how, during our time together,
hours felt like eternal seconds
and were over too quickly.

I live in the sweet sorrow of our parting,

but I hope for an eventual reunion.

Only then may I regain the crest of joy
that radiates from your soul.

00:09

Your gaze upon me,
a bolt of lightning—
shocking and enthralling.

An involuntary tremor
goes through my spine
with your sensual saunter.

Excitement builds
with the dwindling distance
between us.

We wrap each other
in a deep embrace
and I exhale my held breath.

Your body is a toned
muscular majesty,
a temple of perfection.

My heartbeat syncs
with your rhythm

as the scent of honeyed lilacs
drifts from your hair.

This snapshot of heaven
etches into my deepest memory.

00:08

After laying my head on the pillow,
I pull the covers to my chin
and close my eyes.

With an effort,
I clear my mind of all thought
and release my ego.

The hum of white noise
creeps into the remaining vacuum
as I drift towards a Zen state.

The water of delight floods my brain,
and my internal senses are overwhelmed
with your presence.

In this moment of vulnerability,
where I am devoid of self,
you appear.

Even when I try to let go,
you are my constant mind companion.

00:07

In the garden of my mind,
I gaze at the flower of your refinement.

I cultivate the image
and fertilize it with my thoughts.

I will never pluck your bloom.
Instead, I will let it grow and flourish.

00:06

I love the spark between us.
I love the infinity of your embrace.
I love the way you dance:

the flow of your body,
the flash of your eyes,
the smile of your face.

You glow of perfection.

I miss seeing you,
I miss touching your skin,
I miss kissing your lips.

As light is pulled into a black hole,
I am drawn towards your spirit.

I hope to bathe in your essence again
and fill the void of my soul.

Your presence makes me feel alive.
You embody magick!

00:05

A soft whisper
echoes in your ear:
"You are beautiful."

The sound flows from my mouth
as my lips brush against your cheek.
A cherry blossom perfume wafts into my nose.

With our pulses beating in sync,
our hands intertwine.
Hearts merge as one.

Time freezes.
Nothing matters
except this moment.

00:04

Since you are far away,
I close my eyes
and drift into my mind…

The warmth of your skin glows
with an intoxicating vetiver scent.

I taste the swell of your parted lips
and feel their quiver.

The pressure of our bodies increase
as my tongue penetrates.

My fingers flow through silk,
becoming embedded in your hair.

Completely absorbed in the moment,
the outside world disappears.
My focus is you.

00:03

You are the flower of my life—
a wild rose growing
in the tundra of my soul.

Gazing from afar,
I watch as your petals
open in the silvery moonlight.

I feel the essence of love radiate.
It spreads with the warmth of your smile
and the chime of your voice.

I want to be the rich loam
that nurtures and supports you—
a foundation for your hopes and dreams.

Let me be near you
and bask in your light.

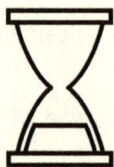

00:02

I think about kissing you
and wonder if your lips still feel the same:

a soft parting firmness that yields
and allows me to breathe of your breath.

With my eyes closed,
I can feel your body pulsating.

Our mouths open
and our tongues dance.

This is how we commune
and get closer to God.

Kissing you is Heaven
and my gateway to eternity.

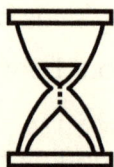

00:01

You are my passion project.

I cannot explain why,
but you have drawn me
into the vortex of your soul.

You have an untouchable quality
that attracts me and fills me with desire.

I am aware that our relationship
may not extend further than the written word.
If I'm lucky, it's a fleeting moment together.

But I have hope;
I have hope for the future.

No matter what happens,
you will always be part of me…

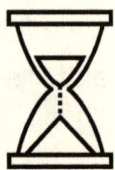

∞

We stand in the doorway
and say goodbye.

I take you in my arms,
close my eyes,
and kiss you.

I kiss you with my entire body.
I drain my essence into your lips.

At the kiss' end,
I look into your eyes
and I am drawn into you.

Oh my God!
I cannot let you go!

I hold you tighter
and kiss you again,
relishing every second.

"Stay with me.

Spend the night," I say.

"I can't," you reply.

With lingering hands,
we say goodnight
and goodbye.

Like dawn climbing through an overcast sky,
a confusing mix of happiness
and sorrow flows through me.

About the Author

Andrew John Chiniche is a self-published author and poet with a vision to add magick to his readers' lives through the power of poetic storytelling. On his lifelong quest of higher truth, he also strives to embolden deep-rooted emotions, inspire deep thought, and invite others to ponder the mysteries of this expansive universe. In addition to authoring five poetry collections (*Love's Dawn*, *Gaze the Moon*, *The Ring of Azurmus*, *Remembrance of Beauty, and Eternal Seconds*), he holds a Bachelor's degree in English Literature from Mississippi State University. When he isn't writing, Andrew enjoys getting lost in the unique worlds of movies and books.